WHEN A BLACK MAN CRIES

THE REVISED VERSION

DR. PAUL J. PORTERFIELD

ZCP

DEDICATION

I dedicate this book to my sons, natural and spiritual, the many men I've counseled, helped, prayed for, and fathered down through the years. May you cry until you see your way again.

CONTENTS

INTRODUCTION

The purpose of this book is not to create a civil uprising; it is not a call to arms for Black America, nor is it a dissertation promulgating the demise of the white race or attacking any race for that matter. It is, though, a wake-up call for the Black man. I am talking to the African American man who has conformed to the mindset of "Black"; one who has said and accepted that he is negative, low, without color, light, and full of ignorance, who has no hope.

This book is designed to stir up the gifts in the Black man so that he can begin to develop into the man inside of him. It may make some men furious, both black and white. Nevertheless, truth often evokes hidden emotions. I wrote this book to give you a signed permission slip to begin your journey that only your tears can take you on. As you read, you will cry because of your many mistakes. However, many of your mistakes were made because there were no men to guide you, no men to say to you, "Stop", because you're hurting, and when you're hurting, you will hurt others.

It is my prayer that if you find yourself angered by the words of this book, you will continue to rebel against the status quo and dare to be different. Please allow the words of this treatise to change the way you look and see, either yourself or your neighbor. Change what you see so that you begin to cry.

CHAPTER 1

WHAT IS A BLACK MAN?

"Black man cleans the streets but mustn't walk freely on the pavement; Black man must build houses for the white man but cannot live in them; Black man cooks the white man's food but eats what is left over. Don't listen to anyone bluff you and say Black and white are brothers."

— Es'kia Mphahlele

Black is a color, not a nationality, not a race. If then that is true, there are not many true black men by color. I am forced to believe that any man can be considered a black man because of the definition of black: Of the very darkest color owing to the absence of or complete absorption of light; the opposite of white. This blackness would be considered the ignorance that many are living in today.

PSALM 119:130

The entrance of thy words giveth light; it giveth understanding unto the simple.

Light is intelligence and wisdom; the natural agent that stimulates sight and makes things visible, being connected to the mental faculty, bright as opposed to dull or ignorant. If we look at the number of men in this society who walk around devoid of light, then there is a great number of black men in the world. They are black because of the ignorance which is grossly accepted and even perpetuated by society. Is it possible for a man of European, Asian, Scandinavian, or not of African descent to be a black man? This is a question that must be integrated into any discussion of or on black men.

A black man could be any man who is ignorant or unlearned, whether by choice or circumstance. This man can be any man who continues to live in this world devoid of the light of understanding when confronted with the truths of the world we live in and the atrocities that present themselves each day. A black man is any man who chooses to live in a constant state of obscurity, without regard to his environment and what takes place around him. Also, a man might be considered black, if, when in receipt of knowledge, he determines through that knowledge that he, himself, is without hope.

Therefore, contrary to popular opinion, a black man is not just a man who has dark brown skin, or a man who is of African descent, but any man who has come to the place in his life where, through the rejection of knowledge, has lost his light, and, as a result, he has lost his hope. That man, brown, yellow, red, or white, is black.

If we are addressing the phrase "black man" as an idiomatic, then unfortunately, only men of my race can be considered as Black men, and it is impossible for any other race or creed to be discussed in the context of a Black man. Black men have been forced to endure because of the interpolation of prejudice and the atrocities of racial and social injustices. In our society, it is essential to address this matter.

"Hope itself is like a star- not to be seen in the sunshine of prosperity, and only to be discovered in the night of adversity."
— Charles H. Spurgeon

Hope is essential for life. This world offers no hope to a man that has been stripped of his pride, dignity, and an ability to provide for his family. Hope says, "If you hold on, it will get better." It takes hope to lie down in your bed, on someone's couch, or even on a piece of cardboard under the highway overpass, and then get up the next morning. The fact that an individual speaks concerning a tomorrow suggests that they have hope.

But, what of that man whose life has gone so far down that he wishes for the cold grip of death during his night season, the man who sees no vision of change in his view of his tomorrow, or that man who has no hope? That man is black. This book is addressed and prayerfully written to all those black men; RED, YELLOW, BLACK, OR WHITE.

The Biblical patriarch, Job, the perpetual voice of hope, is stated in the Holy Scriptures.

JOB 30:30

My skin is black upon me, and my bones are
burned with heat.

The story of Job is one of the most prominent and yet poignant stories of calamity and hope in print. It portrays a man of great notoriety and fame, a man in right relationship with God (the supreme being), who is subsequently turned over to the hand of satan, (the ruler of darkness) by God, to prove that a man can acquire great wealth, and then lose it all, and still be a man of integrity, hope, and faith. Some of the greatest Biblical scholars and many of today's popular Theologians hold that it was the dark and terribly demonstrative circumstances of Job's life that reduced him to becoming a manic depressant. The things that he endured at the hand of satan, made him refer to himself as being black. The seemingly unending cloud of darkness descended upon him and wrought massive destruction in and on his life and family.

As a result of this terrible reign of catastrophic events and the traumatic upheaval in his life, Job lost everything he had.

Is this not what we are seeing today? Many men, any man, rich, poor, African American, Hispanic, Caucasian, can be sitting on a pedestal of prosperity and prominence one day, only to be toppled by life, ending up in the dunghills of impoverishment. There are many who say, "That will never happen to me." However, history bears record that many of the people in this country have experienced this. Our street corners, the prison system, and our homes reveal this. You can be up and abounding one day and then, without warning, down and destitute the next.

A man, while in the heat of oppression and the throws of calamity, can lose his sense of hope. It is this loss of hope which creates a perplexity so overwhelming that all around him appears dark and bleak, black, devoid of light. Hence, Job said, "my skin is black." We should be grateful that, according to the Bible, Job's latter end was far better than his beginning, which releases a ray of hope.

In the Holy Scriptures, Prophet Jeremiah writes about the children of Israel as being a people who had come upon a time of hopelessness. I believe that any race of people who find themselves in a situation of hopelessness are destined to do whatever it takes in order that they might survive. Survival is critical as it is the means of existence in this world.

Self-preservation is the first law of man, but, hope is the key element to survival.

JEREMIAH 18:12

And they said, There is no hope: but we will walk after our own devices, and we will every one do the imagination of his evil heart.

Hope is the ability to look forward to something with some sense of expectation. Any man living without hope is a man who lives without a tomorrow in his thought process. The children of Israel found themselves in a state void of hope. As a result, they resigned themselves to walking after their own devices. It was this decision that caused God to move against them in anger.

Every day of our lives, we see and sense this display of despair. Men, void of hope, operating in their own devices in order that they might survive. Whether the devices are labeled as drugs, alcohol, sexual deviance, illegal practices, or whatever, all these things are what a man might partake or participate in so that he might survive. Not only that, but men who cannot see a way to provide for themselves and their families allow their imaginations to create other evil plans of deception, which they use to survive.

We must first acknowledge that it is not only African

American men who sell drugs, build liquor stores in poor and poverty-stricken communities, and are convicted of sex crimes, or any crime for that matter. It's men period. It, therefore, adds more credence to the above statement and validates the premise that any man can be a black man. Any man void of hope, without a tomorrow, and who has sunk to a state where he will do whatever he must to survive, must be considered a black man.

We are taught to see every American male of African descent as being Black. However, I contend that a black man is not black because of the color of his skin, but he can and should be classified as a black man because of his circumstances and the content of his heart. I consider his circumstances because any man void of hope responds to his daily situations with a gloomy disposition and a departure from his morals. He feels as if nothing he does is going to change where he is. Therefore, he responds not from his character, but from his circumstances and the content of his heart because he lives in a constant state of discontent. All his heart knows is desperation and hopelessness. He cannot see within himself a vision to effect the necessary change and, therefore, operates out of his emotions or heart.

PROVERBS 29:18

Where there is no vision, the people perish...

King Solomon, acclaimed to have more wisdom than anyone, made this statement: without a vision, an individual will perish. So, considering the previous passage of text, we can understand the reasoning for the title of this book. If you cannot see your true surroundings, have no immediate or long-term vision of how to change, and cannot perceive a way to break out of your present situation, you will succumb.

So then, black man, cry. Cry until you wash away the filth of your life; that muck that prevents you from seeing your tomorrows. Cry until the water of your tears dissolves the chains that hold you in the perpetual cycle of despair. Cry until you can see again. Cry until you can see the vision which will thrust you into your destiny. Cry so that you do not perish.

As a man, I am connected to the plight of most men. Let me first say, if it were not for God's grace, I am that man. I am that man who rises day after day and goes to a mundane and unfruitful job, only to receive a paycheck and is unable to pay his bills. I am that man that stands in the shadows and hopes for a brighter day. I am that man who stands on the off-ramps of the highways and panders for bread. I am that man who looks into the eyes of his children with despair, not knowing where the next meal will come from.

Secondly, my life experience has connected me to Asian men who work with all diligence with a goal in mind, only desiring to pull their family along into their prosperity. Life experiences have connected me with European men who have worked hard and made great accomplishments, only to lose it all. My experiences have connected me to African American men who have endured the pain of prejudice and brown men who were judged by the color of their skin. This discrimination could be in the form of a hiring agent in the human resource department refusing to offer a job or promotion, or a police officer racially profiling and arresting a suspect. I have been connected with Hispanic men who only want to have a place in life. I understand the pain of being refused, rejected, and objectified because of my skin color, so I am connected. I have seen the despair of being blackened by the inescapable ways of this world and know the pain that every man endures because of the many mistakes he has made in his life just for being a man.

However, I feel qualified to speak to the African American male because I am an African American male who has withstood the pain of who I am and has figured out that change will come only to those who find God. I have secured a peaceful existence on this planet, and though I have faltered many times along my journey, I have, by the grace of God, survived. The upheavals in my life, the realization of the truth of who I am, and my eyes being opened to the prejudices of this world have afforded me experience in the arena of survival. My experiences have taught me patience and perseverance. I have made many mistakes and have experienced many setbacks, and the pains that come with them. Despite all of the mistakes, setbacks, and pains, God has taught me how to identify the areas of need and discern how to make the changes necessary for survival.

Come with me on this journey and find the place of your tears. I assure you, through the help of God, you will cry, and your life will be changed and changed for the better. It is my hope that all men will read this book and be empowered. However, I want to speak expressly to the African American population of males in this country because I am a product of an African American male who experienced the prejudice and subjugation of life from this world. I come from that broken African American home, that statistically was supposed to produce a negative and non-productive male, and I turned the tables and survived. So, African American men, please read and do not be afraid to gain knowledge from my experience. To all the other men who are reading this book and have not cast it down yet, please continue to read, because knowledge is power.

The male of the African American race has been subjected to the prejudices and atrocities of small-minded and ignorant people more than any other race on this planet. This is not to suggest, by any stretch of the imagination, that other nationalities of men are not currently facing similar situations. I believe that unless you stand or can stand where a man stands, it is almost impossible to understand his plight.

Now, allow me to quiet the mouths of all the naysayers who continue to herald the hyperbole that this country is full of possibilities and that it's out there if you want it, etc. The truth of the matter is, for the African American male, that may not be as true as some would have you think. I harmonize with those who are preaching and heralding prosperity and wealth. I concur that this country is a land that flows with milk and honey, which is one reason why everybody wants to come to America. However, if you don't come in with the mindset that I am willing to fight and slay the giants that already live in this land, you will never be a partaker of the fruit, the milk, or the honey. You will only become one of the tillers of the soil and work as a slave to provide for everyone else's prosperity.

You must be willing to see life as it really is. Stop being deceived by the powers that be. You must know how to handle the ups and downs that come with a sincere pursuit of the prosperity that is out there. And lastly, African American man, you have to recognize that you are not the chosen race. You pose a threat to the establishment and their perception of what is right. Therefore, anything you get will come with a struggle and a fight. You can have it, but you will cry many times before you secure it.

I write this book not as an author, but as an Apostle to the African American race. Having received a spiritual insight from God regarding the real issues, I approach them honestly and prayerfully. Please read this book with an open mind and allow the truth to prevail.

CHAPTER 2

CRYING

There always seems to be something looming over the horizon - something in life that shakes you to your very core. What has your life presented to you that has caused you to cry? I am not saying I want you to cry. However, I am saying it is okay to cry. You can never become so hard that you don't allow your emotions to have that place of pouring out.

One night, while I was resting in my bed, my phone rang. A young man was on the other end, facing a major ordeal in his life. Through the cracking in his voice and the hesitation in his words, he made a statement that brought a question to my mind. He confessed, "I just feel like crying." Having experienced the pain of the same ordeal, I patiently replied, "Go ahead, son. Go ahead and cry."

I knew that the experience of crying would be the genesis of his release, which would ultimately be the beginning of his being able to get through this terrible ordeal. Listening to him as he quietly wept as if trying to hold on to his dignity as a man, I interrupted and said, "No, son. I mean, it's alright to cry. Cry." Then, he began to exude sounds of pain and brokenness. He cried like an injured child. Sitting there, I began to search my mind as to why. Why do mature, professional, and prosperous men feel as if they need approval to cry?

After being allotted time to cry, while he spoke to me through his tears, I could hear his fears and doubts, his concerns about his manhood, about who he was, and even his despair as to where he was going in his life. As we continued our conversation, I could hear him speaking, a more confident man, a man who began to realize that what had happened to him had happened to many other men. As he began to reach conclusions about what he needed to do to resolve the situation, he began the healing process. We had prayer and ended the call.

As I sat there pondering the situation, the call, and its results, I wondered: Just as this young man needed to cry, how many more men in the world needed to cry? Secondly, why is it that men feel the need to seek out permission to cry? And finally, why does it seem so taboo for an African American man to cry?

I can remember many times throughout the difficult and tumultuous years of my life, I, too, wanted to cry. I wouldn't, however, maybe even couldn't because I had been raised to believe the fallacy that big boys didn't cry, especially African

American boys. I was raised to believe that crying was a sign of weakness, and growing up in an environment where you didn't or couldn't show any signs of weakness for fear of being beaten or worse, I taught myself not to cry. Nevertheless, there were many times when I really wanted to cry.

I wanted to cry when I considered my mother, a single black woman who was forced to be a mother and a father, a young woman with no other alternative than to do it alone. She struggled to raise and provide for me and still had no inheritance to leave to me. My mother was a nurse who worked hard at a rehabilitation hospital in Philadelphia, Pennsylvania. I would watch her get up early every morning to trek off to that hospital to work her shift, sometimes working overtime because she wanted to fill the voids. Then, I would watch painfully as she returned home, so tired and drained that she could barely stand to cook dinner. I wanted to cry for her.

I wanted to cry because of the emptiness that I always felt. My mother was forced to take on a role she was unprepared for. She had to become the provider. Because she had to take the place of the man in my life and become the provider, every day after school, I would have to come home to an empty house. The emptiness of the house only intensified the emptiness I experienced in my heart. The emptiness of a broken home, a home without a man inside its walls.

It was not just an empty home. There were empty seats at

the table, so there was no family discussion at the end of the day. The living room had an empty recliner, meaning there was no male impartation. There was an empty place in her bedroom, so I never realized the need for a man to be there.

Integral parts of my growth were missing. This forced me to abort a portion of my childhood and grow up prematurely, creating in me a void that had to be filled at some point in my life. Now, some other woman would be burdened with the task of finishing the assignment given to my mother. Although my mother taught me manners and respect, she couldn't teach me that from a man's point of view.

Because of her pain, she taught me pain. Through her frustration, she taught me frustration. I watched her live in survival mode, so I, too, began living in a constant state of survival mode. She taught me how to never give up and how to survive, but unfortunately, she never taught me how to live.

Many young men today are being forced to grow up prematurely, unable to live out their young lives. They were never completely raised to adulthood, which means some other woman will be beleaguered with dealing with the unfinished product. Someone other than the mother will end up having to raise this wounded and broken child. Just because a man is 30, 40, or maybe even 50 doesn't mean he has matured. It simply means he has grown up. This is the ongoing plight of men, not just African American men. Men are entering into their manhood unraised and incomplete, so they are passing this on to the men they are creating and the cycle of broken homes begins.

Let's get back to the crying. You don't always know what a man cries about. I wanted to cry because of the failed marriages that occurred in my life, the ridicule, and the ex-communication I experienced because of them. Many of my peers who grew up with me in the church looked at me negatively because of the broken state I existed in. And as a result, they decided to disassociate themselves from me. This left me alone to try to figure this out on my own. The problem was, or so I thought, that there was no man to instruct me. I didn't realize that instructions were being imparted; they were just the wrong type.

There was one man, though, my spiritual leader, who I thought was the pattern from which I would be cut. I respected and loved him. However, his extramarital affair with one of my older sisters taught me an inaccuracy. Through his weakness, I learned an inaccurate behavior. I learned that it was satisfactory to have sex outside of the marriage bond, and I operated out of that fallacy because it was self-pleasing.

There was no man to show me how to be real with myself and my mate, to discuss the issues that threatened the relationship, even if it meant crying. Because of that, I went through a part of my life hurting and broken. This brokenness wasn't good for my relationships. It destroyed many.

Because of the failed marriages, I thought there was a problem with my sexual prowess. This only exacerbated the problem and perpetuated the cycle of adultery and fornication. I was trying to prove to myself that there was nothing wrong with me, which took me further away from God. Instead of identifying the true issue, I began studying the female psyche and her anatomy, and from that, I learned how to satisfy and please a woman mentally, physically, and sexually. Still, none of these things resolved the ongoing, seemingly never-ending issue. It was not enough to become perfect in one or two areas and still be incomplete in other areas. Without failing or making mistakes, it is almost impossible to learn the correct way of doing a thing. So now, I have learned to embrace every failure of my past and find the lesson.

I wanted to cry because of the children that I fathered, whom I had severed myself from and longed to connect with. You see, to the person who looked on from the outside, it appeared that I didn't want anything to do with my children, which was not the case. I am pleased to say that crying allowed me to correct many of the issues I had with my children, and we are now working on relationships.

Fathers have a spiritual responsibility to impart to their children. Not being able to do so will create an internal sickness known only to the father. I know there are fathers who are reading this book, and you have children outside of your current marriage or relationship. It is alright for you to cry concerning those children. If your spouse or partner is unaware of them, make it known, and cry together if you must. The crying will allow you to begin the process of healing. It will open the door to the desire to connect. You may not connect, but at least there will no longer be the void of not knowing.

We tend to discredit the missing father in the scenario because it is often impossible to know the true heart of the man involved. In many cases, things are not always as they appear. And if you are a man who has a father who has not connected with you, for whatever reason, cry, allow the process of healing to begin, and make the opportunity available. It may be that he is crying as well.

As I began writing this book in 2011, I was unaware of my hidden unresolved issues that had not been dealt with. One day, I began to cry and continued in my tears for a few days, which felt like a lifetime. It was during this time that I began to understand the importance of my tears. My tears uncovered two of my major issues: One, I had not dealt with my failed relationships, which thrust me into more unhealthy relationships. I had not stopped, evaluated, observed, and acknowledged what made the relationships fail. Without this, I would have perpetuated the same patterns and made the same mistakes. Secondly, I had not connected to the children I had fathered, and it left a void. From this, I fathered more children, but I could not connect with them. Without the connection to the children we have fathered, we will only create a desire to father other children, subconsciously trying to fill that void that exists from our missing children.

Finally, I wanted to cry for all the mistakes I had made in my life; mistakes with women, mistakes in my ministry, and mistakes in managing my money. Many of my mistakes were because there was no man to guide me, to inform me that crying does not change the fact that I am a man, or to say to me, "You're hurting, and it's alright to cry." Understand, I make no excuses. These are just the realities of my life. However, since there was no one to permit me to cry, I held back many tears, and my tears were the containers of the pain I carried.

This was more devastating to me than I knew. The horrendous and maturing pain that I harbored inside was only fostering and creating demons. These evil forces were stripping the power from me to hear my intellect, subjecting me to situations that were even worse than those that I needed to cry about.

There is no wisdom in putting off things that can be done, remedied, or resolved right away. You need to pause, look back over your life, determine where you need to cry and ascertain if you still need that cry. You must deal with these hidden issues.

CHAPTER 3

SLAVERY

When we open the dialogue on slavery, we automatically ascribe to the African American populace and not mankind in general. Slavery is that system which promotes the owning of an individual by another individual. If that is the case, then slavery does truly exist today and must be mentally eradicated from the minds of men and physically removed from the social order of our country. Ultimately, any person who is forced into situations against their will, without the ability to flee, is a slave. People are slaves to unfair business practices, their jobs, businesses, and even marriages. Then there are the horrible trends of sex and drug slaves.

The one thing I usually hear at the beginning of discussions concerning the Black race and the condition of its people is, "Well, what will it take for the people to heal?" Some people shout reparations for the past, and others cry, "We need our own lands." I am convinced that until we discuss slavery in its entirety across every color and sexual barrier, there can be no true resolution for slavery, for any people.

We must remove the multicolored tapestry that has been woven concerning this great country, the ugly thread that has been intertwined into the patchwork of this society for ages. This country's heritage has been marred by an ugly, stench-filled boil called slavery. In this country, freedom was one of the founding principles set forth by whom I believe were hypocritical fathers of the Constitution. Freedom does not produce slavery, but it was birthed, nurtured, and allowed to remain in America. It is merciless and continued through centuries; unfortunately, it still exists in 2023.

Slavery against the Black race was outlawed in 1865 by an amendment to the Constitution. However, because slavery was and still is a luxury for the wealthy, it still exists. Not necessarily as we knew it, but certainly, slavery is still here. And until we as a people honestly acknowledge it, from the White House to the smallest shack in the field, slavery will continue to be a festering sore on the backside of this country.

There may no longer be African men and women living on plantations, being forced to endure the painful, torturous whip of the slave master, or the horrendous acts of violence disseminated against them. However, the Black man is still being treated like a slave, a second-class citizen, with no value other than to serve his master. He may not live on the plantation, but he lives in the prison. He may no longer be being whipped with a bullwhip, but he is still being beaten into submission. You may not see the atrocious images of black bodies hanging on trees, but Black men are still being hung. It may not be by the hands of the master that the Black man is being castrated, but in truth, castration is still a reality, especially amongst African American males.

How can we live in an age so technologically advanced and still see slavery in this country? This is America, the land of the free and the home of the brave. Or was it all a lie? As a human being, you should be appalled. The thought of men and women in the throws of life, unable to live according to the tenets of the Constitution. That in itself should make you cry.

Cry

Dr. P. Jonathan Porterfield's Definition

A Verb

1. Shed tears, especially as an expression of distress or pain

2. Crying is the act of shedding tears, allowing the salty liquid, that is produced by the lacrimal gland, to moisten the cornea, and cleanse the eye.

Tears

What is this coming out of my eye? What is this liquid falling from my eyes? These are tears. I don't understand this. I'm crying. I don't do this. What's going on with me? Is my manhood in question? Men who have grown up under the impression that they shouldn't cry will deal with some of these same questions.

There were times when I wanted to cry, but I wouldn't. I held back many tears. I learned that my tears were essential to becoming a real man. Men, you must acknowledge that you are hurt and cry. It's alright to cry. I want to tell you that crying does not change the fact that you are a man. Men need to cry just as much as anyone else. The reality for many men is that no one has been there for them to release "that" part of their life to. You must know that you are not alone in this.

An individual will shed tears due to a piece of foreign matter in the eye or a strongly felt emotion such as distress or heart pain. Most of the time, when something is in the eye until it produces tears, the individual becomes temporarily or partially blinded. Is there something in your eye preventing you from seeing clearly, perhaps some foreign matter? Is there something going on in your psyche, whether from your past or present, that is causing you enough pain that you feel it necessary to have this outward display of emotions? It could be a habit that has taken control of your life. Perhaps it is a relationship that has turned into an emotional rollercoaster. Maybe it's a personal objective that has become so obsessive that you can no longer see clearly. Have you allowed a foreign object to become an irritant to your vision?

The problem with the irritant is you cannot prevent crying. You will cry, guaranteed. Allow the tears to come. Let your tears acknowledge some form of disturbance that has affected your state of calm or your ability to see. If you don't cry, no one will know, and you will either be forced to deal with it yourself, or you will remain hopelessly in a state of pain and blindness. If you want to help yourself to be free of the entanglements, you must first acknowledge that there is some form of mental or spiritual disturbance.

Your acknowledgment is in the form of your tears. I am not using crying as a metaphor. I refer to the crying with which we all are familiar: the shedding of tears. It is my conviction that the streaming tears of a Black man serve a dual purpose. The tears do not just run down from his eye merely to show his pain or that his peace has been disturbed, but they also burn a thoroughfare in his heart and furrow out within himself a passageway of escape so that he might evade his present conjuncture. His tears clear his mental faculty of all the murky waters of life, which cover the road he travels and reveal to him a way to abscond. Even more importantly, they turn him back to the God of his foreparents. The God he knows, the God with which he is, or should be, familiar with. The God that brings him freedom from the slavery of the mental and spiritual disturbance.

As you read this book, you may begin to realize how lost and lonely you really are. However, your Heavenly Father is waiting to comfort and heal you. Reach out to Him. He will hear your cry, and His word promises that He will wipe all of your tears away. It is my hope that as you read this book, you will acknowledge your need to cry and, even more so, your need for God.

Crying, you say, it's not for me. You insist that you have no need to cry. You also believe that crying is just an external show of internal emotions and that you don't need everyone to know how you really feel. Hiding your true emotions and feelings will only build walls around your heart. And as unfortunate as that may be, most men have lived a lifetime hiding their feelings. However, I contend that when a Black man cries, he not only opens the door of his heart, but he also opens all of the other sensory gates.

His tears reveal the true state of his life and the bitter taste of the tainted meat he's consumed to survive. It expresses the cries of the generations who have passed on before him—men such as the Hispanic men who were enslaved by poverty because of their inability to achieve naturalization, the African American men who were wrongfully and viciously enslaved, hung by the neck, brutally castrated due to the sexual depravity of their white owners, and the Jewish men who were mistreated because of their heritage. All of these nationalities of men gave their lives so that men could comprehend and enjoy what was called their inalienable rights. Men, we must cry to cleanse our sight of these foreign matters of our lives.

The Sons of Kings & Queens

It has been said that knowledge is power. However, knowledge in the wrong hands can be the most destructive agent. What you know about yourself can build and strengthen you and even change the course of your life. However, keep in mind, that same knowledge in someone else's hands could be used to destroy you.

The fact that a good percentage of Black men and women can trace their bloodlines back to royalty presents an unequal part of the equation that cannot be resolved with normal mathematical calculations. You must allow your mind to embrace the fact that what you are is not determined by where you are. We have allowed our circumstances to dictate our environment and our environment to dictate our conscious thought. You can live on the poorest block in the neighborhood and be the most intelligent child. Yet, if you allow your environment to hold your mind, your intelligence is wasted.

It is for this reason that we become successful drug dealers. We have the intelligence to see a way out of our situation, but allow our environment to hold us as opposed to escaping. On the flip side of that coin, you can live on the most affluent block, walking and talking with millionaires daily, but your ignorance will cause your fall.

Who Will Cry

I feel there is another definition of crying that must be interjected at this point; it is "a public demand". The world must demand a voice that will openly and honestly declare that the Black man, whether he is African, Jewish, Caucasian, Hispanic, or Oriental, is lost. We have negated the presence of this brokenness and, as a result, have perpetuated the lost state. He is consumed in the vicious cycle of life, continuing in a revolving door of endless disappointments and consequences: slavery.

There is an imminent danger looming in the darkness of society. A weird and senseless setting of death and destruction because of the lack of a voice. Most men seem to have a wolf-pack mentality, of which there is nothing wrong. It means that we, as men, can be a powerful force, but we require a lead wolf. Someone willing to step to the front of the pack and lead.

The problem in the past has been that if anyone would dare do that, they were assassinated. So, what we hear are single small voices crying out, showing the atrocities, but backing up and hiding in the pack for fear of being killed. Who will cry? We have watched great men step to the forefront of the struggle and pull us out. Nevertheless, before the task is completed, we have seen them murdered to squelch the uprising.

Slave masters of old used the same technique on their plantations. They would castrate or mutilate anyone who would seek to be free to erase from another's mind that desire. There is a hope in this writer's heart that some men would say, "If you go, I'll follow, cover, and protect you." But until that time, like John the Baptist, I'll be the voice of one crying in the wilderness.

Of African Descent and Wealthy

Wealth is not something that is often ascribed to African men, because it is hard for most Caucasian men to believe that men of color should have or that they have the propensity to acquire wealth. The common thread through the destruction of African American wealth was the thought that African American men were mentally challenged and unable to maintain their wealth. So, the European man was determined to systematically remove the wealth and the appetite for wealth from the African American man, which has served to stifle the rebirth of wealth in African American families. This has also perpetuated the lie, which has been the ongoing thought process of white men in America. That lie is that African American men are unqualified to have anything because he is intrinsically imprudent and, therefore, incapable of mentally devising and maintaining a source of wealth.

When history portrays men of wealth, they always illustrate the Caucasian male, milky white in color and stern-faced, which visually says that white men can make money, protect money, and should always have money. I submit to you that it is not the color of your complexion that provides you with the mental capacity to acquire wealth. It is indeed a truth that any man, black, white, or anywhere in between, can have the mental ability to get wealth. However, there must be a cognitive understanding of wealth and an intellectual appreciation of what it can do. Again, any man can acquire wealth. However, the record could reflect a different imagery. Again, any man can acquire wealth.

However, the record could reflect a different imagery. If

Job lived in this era, he would be a very affluent man. In his time, he was considered to be the richest man in the land. However, I would like to address the statement, "My skin is black...". (Job 30:30) Could it possibly be that the wealthiest man in the land at that time was a Black man? Could it be that God allowed Satan to test the integrity of the man whom He had such reverence for? Or perhaps this man experienced so much trouble and emotional pain that his skin dried up and turned black? Or finally, is it possible that his skin turned black as a result of the mental despair and physical sickness that he endured?

CHAPTER 4

THE BLACK BUCK SYNDROME

The "Black Buck Syndrome" is a state of being that I have identified and labeled because of the continued rise of single mothers in Black America. I use this phrase because it brings to mind a serious problem that faces the Black man and, ultimately, the Black race: the birthing of children to unwed parents. I believe this chapter will be a great help to Black men, as well as Black women. It will assist in analyzing a problem they deal with in their everyday lives. I hope that as this chapter is read, eyes are opened to the truth.

A syndrome is a series of things that form a pattern, a group of things or events that form a recognizable pattern, especially of something undesirable. A slavery mentality still exists in America and has become a syndrome of destruction. I recognize it as a syndrome because it follows a specific pattern. A pattern is a guide from which things are reproduced. However, if the pattern is flawed, everything created from the pattern also is flawed.

A myriad of conferences and seminars were set up and

intended to address the question: How can we stop or prevent the continued rise in children being born among young single women in the Black populace? From the various conferences and seminars, we have seen numerous programs launched, spanning from free condom distribution to classes on planned parenting implemented only to no avail. In addition, as unfortunate as it is, the age of single mothers is becoming younger and younger each year. We have reached a plateau where children are having children. Moreover, it seems that there is no hope of turning.

Let me remind you, though, that knowledge is power. In light of the fact that this is a delicate area, allow me to share with you the reason I feel we have this dilemma. The information I share with you will produce knowledge, giving you the power to create change.

The pattern of reproduction in Black America has been marred because of the Black Buck Syndrome; the pattern, which once required two loving, committed individuals, now only requires two sex partners. What was once loving, referred to as "we are having our baby" is now mentioned in a comic discourse: "That girl done gone and got pregnant."

We see this problem in every race; it is just not as open. It is imperative that we address it in the Black population. I would not say that the birth of any child is a problem. However, I contend that birthing children in unfavorable conditions is not conducive to the successful rearing of strong Black men and women. Although many children from single parent families have grown to become great men and women, we should not allow the success to deceive us into thinking that it is okay to perpetuate this type of lifestyle.

The Black Buck Syndrome is a metaphor that I often use to explain the promiscuity of the Black race. It is in no way an excuse or a license to engage in sexual activity with reckless abandon. It is simply to help the reader understand how we have come to be where we are.

Allow your mind to go back to a time of immense exploitation of African males and females. It was a time in history when African men and women were enslaved. A time in which African men and women were inflicted with numerous sufferings and tremendous pain, savagely removed from their homes, and violently removed from their lands. Africans were forced to live in deplorable conditions that were not acceptable for men or beasts. It encompasses a time when African human beings were treated worse than animals. They were brought to this newly formed country to be slaves to disgraceful Caucasian men and women who cared for their animals more than they did the people they had enslaved. These owners demanded work and production from African men and women, some of whom were royalty. Only to pay them with senseless beatings and, for many, death for those who could not produce.

Then consider with me, if you would please, the problem facing these plantation owners. His land has begun flourishing because of the Blacks that were being used as laborers, however, the slaves were dying out. He observed that the stronger laborers could withstand more abuse and still manage to work and produce. It was a fact the stronger the labor, the greater the harvest. In his mind, he realized that to maintain the success he was experiencing, he needed to produce the strong and decrease the weak. So, a plan was conceived in his mind. He would pick the largest, strongest buck (the name of the Black field hand) he could find and would send him in with the strongest young winch (the name of the Black woman) on the plantation to copulate with and eventually impregnate to breed and maintain strong workers on his plantation.

There was no love involved. Both parents knew it was about breeding, so they remained detached and severed from the act. After a while, because of the ability of the Black man to adapt, it was made to feel all right. Their adaptation was based on the premise of hope. Those Black men and women hoped that one of the children they produced would one day grow up and become their liberator and set them free.

This set off within the women an internal security system, as it were. Through the continual birthing of these children, the mothers and fathers began evolving. Every mother has within her an internal instinct to protect and nurture her off-spring. The instinct, coupled with the natural ability to adapt, created a void. Without the help of the slave who fathered the child and without the acceptance of the slave owner, the mothers recognize the need to be a father as well. These women raised their children and taught them how to survive without a man. They instilled in them a lack of need for the father. They did not want the children to become dependent upon a non-existent father, unsure as to whether the father of the child would be there or not.

The African women were forced to adapt to this terrible treatment. Failure to comply only meant severe beatings and possible expulsion from the plantation. It also could mean separation from the only family she had or knew of. There-fore, as a result, she grew strong in her resolve to raise the children born from these encounters and make them as strong and independent as she was.

When the Black men began loving the Black women and trying to protect them and their children, they were sold off to other Plantation owners. Without the support and love of the father, the families begin forming a dysfunctional mentality. Families begin feeling and believing that they could survive without the man in the house. They were forced to survive this because of the tendency to remove the men from the house. Either the Black father was sold off to another plantation for rebellion or was murdered.

On the other hand, the white father would not or could not acknowledge his child born of a slave, not in the parental sense. He would acknowledge within himself that he had created a life. However, he was not willing to be a father. As a result, it became all right for the mother to raise children alone and without a father. It also came to be accepted. As a result, the children began accepting it as the way it should be. When in reality, it was never the plan. The child should never have to grow up without the love and guidance of their father and the love and nurturing of their mother. This set in motion the Black Buck Syndrome.

Why are there so many single parents in Black America? How is it that a Black man can produce a child and needs the court system to assign him the responsibility of child support for him to provide for the child? The mental capacity of righteousness has been injured or destroyed by fire. Not the fire that burns in the fireplace but the fires of slavery, mistreatment, and prejudice. These fires destroy everything they touch.

The mind has been deceived into thinking like the mind of the past. Men and women are living subconsciously in slavery times and have adapted to the Black Buck Syndrome. Black men are still going into young women's bedrooms and engaging in sex and making babies without connecting the heart, saying, "This is just the way I am." Young Black women are still saying, "I do not need a man to raise my child." Subconsciously, they are still carrying out the orders of the slave masters. They fail to realize that by continuing the practice, they are the perpetrators of the downward spiraling trend of the African Black man.

In the heart of the Black man, he is still trying to sire a deliverer. This statement does not refer to the deliverance of mankind but the deliverer of the Black race. He is not cognizant of the fact that the deliverer of the Black race has already come. It is the Black man himself. Therefore, we have an ongoing condition.

I must stop. Black man, you must cry. Cry and allow the tears to clear your eyes and see who you are. You must see your children as being your inheritance. They are what you leave behind for the world to see as your epitaph.

To my knowledge, there is no documentation as to how the separation of the buck from the child influences the child and the mother, and certainly not how it affects the buck. However, because of the anguish I have often felt personally, I believe there were many nights when that big, strong Black man cried. The man who was ripped from his home, savagely beaten, and horrendously tortured still would not allow his nemesis to see him cry.

Now, the buck sits in darkness. A darkness so thick he

cannot see his life in front of him. He sits in pain and a frustration only he can comprehend, and he begins to cry. A new emptiness has found its way into his heart. He has never experienced so great a magnitude of emptiness, the emptiness that only a father can know because of his missing child.

African men who had been violently removed from their families were made to adjust to the pain of separation. Facing loneliness was customary as men were naturally prepared to leave their homes, however, this was a different loneliness. Somewhere in his heart, he knew that there should have been an offspring. He had left a seed in the womb of a woman. Yet, there was no parental connection. There was no child to embrace. No cry for his protection.

He felt the need within himself to connect with his seed, but there was none. Within his heart, a void existed, and his attempt to nullify the void manifested as sexual prowess. He misunderstood what he was feeling. He thought it was an appetite to receive love when, in reality, it was a desire to give love to his offspring. Moreover, when he could find no satisfaction, the Black man cried.

Many children today have been and still are being reared without the love of a father. They have grown up to be successful men and women. Some have gotten over the hurt that they experienced, and some have not. However, this does not mean the father did not cry for his offsprings many nights.

What it does say is that men need to be educated because the ignorance of their past was so real that it controlled their present life. Children hold on. The fathers are coming back. They are coming back because the fathers have begun to cry.

43

PROBLEM

There is a prevailing fear in mainstream America today. This fear has been the driving force in the continued encumbering of the Black man. What is this fear you ask, and can it be relieved? The fear comes in the form of questions. What if Black men unite under sincere leadership, the kind of leadership that leads by illustration and vision? What would the results be?

On the other hand, what if someone were to step to the forefront and call Black men to arms and raise a nation out of a nation? There would be nothing impossible for them. There was a similar statement about Black men, not out of fear, but as an acknowledgment, by a power far greater than the power that runs this country.

GENESIS 10:8-10

8 *And Cush begat Nimrod: he began to be a mighty one in the earth.* **9** *He was a mighty hunter before the LORD: wherefore it is said, Even as Nimrod the mighty hunter be-*

fore the LORD. **10** *And the beginning of his kingdom*
was Babel, and Erech, and Accad, and Calneh,
in the land of Shinar.

Historians and theologians teach us that Cush was a pre-decessor of the African race. In addition, scriptures in the Holy Bible verify that Nimrod, the son of Cush, was the founder of a kingdom named Babel. The people of that kingdom began a building program to erect a tower to the heavens. Their accomplishment was so profound that it resonates throughout history as "The Tower of Babel" and is infamous because it was there that God separated the Black race into diverse peoples.

GENESIS 11:1-9

1 *And the whole earth was of one language, and of one*
speech. **2** *And it came to pass, as they journeyed from the*
east, that they found a plain in the land of Shinar; and they
dwelt there. **3** *And they said one to another, Go to, let us*
make brick, and burn them throughly. And they had brick
for stone, and slime had they for morter. **4** *And they said,*
Go to, let us build us a city and a tower, whose top may
reach unto heaven; and let us make us a name, lest we be
scattered abroad upon the face of the whole earth. **5** *And the*
LORD came down to see the city and the tower, which the

children of men builded. 6 And the LORD said, Behold, the people is one, and they have all one language; and this they begin to do: and now nothing will be restrained from them, which they have imagined to do. 7 Go to, let us go down, and there confound their language, that they may not understand one another's speech. 8 So the LORD scattered them abroad from thence upon the face of all the earth: and they left off to build the city. 9 Therefore is the name of it called Babel; because the LORD did there confound the language of all the earth: and from thence did the LORD scatter them abroad upon the face of all the earth.

In the birthing of cultural diversity, the Black race is now divided into many nationalities. Moreover, through this, we see the beginning of sorrow for the Black man. I contend that it was here that God determined that if the Black man would ever become completely united as in times past, that nothing that he would imagine to do would be unattainable. It was at that time that God determined to divide the Black race into a myriad of races. From that time, one of the most difficult things to do has been to mobilize the Black race and be as one people. Yet, there is hope.

According to the scriptures, God has a plan for all mankind, and this plan is coming into focus. The scriptures declare in Hosea chapter 2, verse 6, "After two days will he revive us: in the third day he will raise us up, and we shall live in his sight." The interpretation of the scriptures alludes to God's timing: one day is a thousand years, and a thousand years is as one day. If that is the case, then we are in the time of our revival.

I believe we have come through the second day. God has raised us up. We are seeing more African American men and women in the political arena, as well as the business sector, and now, as we are coming into the third day, he has begun the process of reviving us. Thank God we elected an African American President who is constantly in our prayers. However, it is not yet complete because we need men and women on the grassroots level who are willing to lead young Black men and women out of the crack houses and off of the street corners. Lead them back into places of learning, where they can affect change in their lives as well as their children's lives. God must raise leaders from among us in this time that will unite us and thrust us into our destinies.

Black man cry. Cry to God for the leaders that must come and take their places. Cry that they will no longer be controlled by the fear that torments this nation.

By looking at the fear of the nation, we can then comprehend the fear of the Black man. It is this fear that causes white America to fight so vehemently against this race. It is the same fear that promotes racial unrest, prejudice, and discord between the races. It has been said that if the Black man doesn't want to be here, then he should go back to Africa. It is an untruth; the Black man does not want to leave America.

He wants to live here with the same rights and privileges allowed to every other man. Still, every problem usually brings with itself an onslaught of other problems.

The true problem that faces Black America today then is leadership. There is a lack of Black men willing to rise to the call of leadership. Or could it be said that there are not enough Black men capable of leadership? By this, I mean African American men who can withstand the frontal attack that will ensue as a result of a Black man accepting the challenge.

Prior to now, there have been a few African American men who have recognized this need. Black men who have acknowledged the need for change and have made themselves available for leadership have been exterminated before they had the opportunity to effect any real change. This has instilled a fear and created a seemingly insurmountable quandary, but the time that we are living in today calls for Black men who are not just willing to lead, but are willing to die for what they believe.

One of the problems encountered with this is that the individual who steps to the forefront with a vision of unity becomes a target and is neutralized or, inevitably, invalidated by their past. Therefore, the task before us is to nurture genuine leaders who are willing to accept the assignment and unite Black men. Not to establish a cult or a church, not even another movement. Just some individuals who will say as Jesus said, Follow me, and I will make you who you should really be.

CHAPTER 6

SOLUTION

To every problem, there must be a solution. I believe that the "problem" has existed for so long, and there appears to be no solution. However, I also believe we have seen solutions and have ignored them for obvious reasons. We can no longer fear the change that is necessary. The solution is about change.

The solution to this particular problem is to begin training men to be leaders. Genuine leaders are often born from unassuming origins. Therefore, you may not find these men in the Senate or coming out of Law School. They may not be found on the list of America's top 100 Black men of today. They may be me of a lowly degree with a desire to see the race set free.

However, they must be men who can hear the cries and develop an appetite for struggle, because it will be their hunger for true righteousness that will birth a vision of departure. The hunger will awaken them to their surroundings and say to them, "You don't belong here." Therefore, hearing this, they will begin to envision themselves in another place. They will start making statements like "I have a vision" or "I have a dream."

Now, be reminded that two types of men fit the criteria for leaders: the unassuming and the presuming. Both of them have the markings for leadership, but only one will be successful. The unassuming man with true vision tends to be a rebel. He is referenced as a troublemaker. His movements are marked and monitored as an insurgent. This relentless scrutiny inaugurates within him a constant warring against the status quo. He is used as a paradigm to promote fear.

The reason for this attack is so that no one else would dare to advance toward his personal vision. The media sets in on him so that he appears to be untrustworthy. The enforcers of the law handle him with disdain to reduce his credibility. However, his only desire is to help the crying Black men of the time to become who they are to be. He has not led a perfect life because he was not raised with purpose. His purpose was raised in him. Yes, he made mistakes, and maybe he's even in prison. Nevertheless, there is a vision in him that has a destiny. So, when he rises in society, the powers that be send the signal that he must be dealt with immediately to maintain their status quo.

Then there is the other man, the noise maker or the presuming. He creates a cacophony that is deafening and drowns out the true purpose of the position of leadership. However, no one attacks him. No one really wants to shut him up. He becomes the court jester, allowed only to continue making folly. He will never really accomplish much of anything other than drawing attention to himself. He becomes the laugh of the year. You are likely to see his picture in the yearly reviews of the programs that elucidated blunders to remind you of his current condition so that you make no attempts of setting yourself free.

Nevertheless, if the job is to be accomplished, the unassuming man will accomplish it. The quiet man with a loud cry is the person who will get the job done. He is the man with the vision, the one who really comprehends the problem and arrives at an answer. He is the one who, through conspiracy, is removed from the equation. Moreover, he is the one who ends up the target of assassination, but this man must be covered and nurtured so as not to expire before his time.

The true Black man poses no threat of fear. Simply allow him to function in society the way every other man is, and he will be a contribution. Note, I said true Black man. I refer to him in his manner because a true Black man who has seen himself cry and has allowed others to see him cry can open himself enough to be inundated with his purpose and, by that, makes changes to his environment. This man has allowed others to see him and, therefore, can be touched by the needs of others. Only this man can be effective in his assignment. Only this man can be true to who he is, as well as true to others around him.

The Black man I speak of is a man birthed between the thighs of hardship, raised and nurtured on the milk of trials and tribulations, molded and formed by the cruel hand of poverty, and made into a chiseled piece of black granite. He is hardened by his continual rejection yet softened by his hope for change. He is age-wise from his mistakes and yet infantile in his desire to learn. He is sharp with his tongue and yet dull with his fist. This Black man is broken from his many fights with injustice, yet he is whole in his struggles against impartiality. He is abnormally strong, and still, he is not a superman. This Black man is the husband, the son, the father, and the brother. He is every Black man who has ever seen himself and cried.

Now, this will require a transformation, and I can think of no safer place to find support for transformation than in the Holy Scriptures.

ROMANS 12:2

And be not conformed to this world: but be ye transformed by the renewing of your mind, that ye may prove what is that good, and acceptable, and perfect, will of God.

This great transformation cannot take place until the Black man is constrained to see the truth and respond to it mentally and not just physically. He must be confronted with his mindset and be willing to renew his thought process. He must also be prepared to reevaluate his position by hearing the truth, not with the melody of hatred playing quietly in the background or with the drums of uprising pounding in his ears, but with the symphonic resonance of other men crying. The Black man will not comprehend the need for transformation until he hears and feels the plight of his fellow man. He must hear the crying.

Oh, my brother, open your ears and hear the cries. You might not hear sobbing. You may not hear the tear-jerking sounds of crying. You may just hear another man make a statement regarding how many times he has applied for a specific job that he is more qualified to have and still has not been hired. You might hear of another Black man being sent to prison unjustly and of another who has been refused housing in an upscale housing area, nevertheless, you must hear the crying. When these things happen, somewhere in the thick darkness, that man will bend his back, grip his face, and he will cry.

CHAPTER 7

THE PLIGHT OF THE BLACK RACE

The word plight is indicative of the condition of the Black man. He is faced with a terrible predicament. How does he live today for his tomorrows when his yesterdays were so injurious? What must he do to change the direction in which he is headed? Finally, how can he make that change without having a true sense of where he has been?

These questions identify one of the more serious problems facing the current Black American generation. The average young Black man or woman does not know their history. No race of people is less discerning of their history than the African Americans. It is not that the history is not there. It is that we still flinch when it is presented. For that reason, we do not have a desire to deal with it.

I think this can be said of any group of people who have experienced the horrendous misfortune of slavery, genocide, and murder. It hurts to deal with it. Maybe we should stop trying to deal with it and accept it as fact. We need to acquire a true knowledge of accurate accounts so that it does not happen again.

Our young people need to know our history, and I do not think we should wait for February (Black History Month) to discuss it. Four hundred years of lies and mistreatment cannot be rationalized in a month of remembrance. The time of our suffering must be memorialized. It should be rehearsed in our hearing so that it becomes a part of our mentality.

A curriculum should be established that will correlate with the History program already in place.

African Americans should create a curriculum in their homes or churches that addresses African American history. We must acquire knowledge and an awareness of our history. Knowledge of the past is the only true instrument to initiate change for the future. The truth of the past must be sought out with all diligence and fervor.

Empowering our youth with the true knowledge of their past will do more to advance them than any social program. The race is being destroyed from within, because our youth do not know where they come from. They are not aware of the pain that has been inflicted upon the Black race.

Because we have two generations of young people raised by television, most of their knowledge comes from a television program. We watched "Roots," and that became our information source.

I challenge every young Black man to search out his personal history. Learn who in your bloodline was privy to first-hand information because they were there. Ask them to share with you the horrible forms of mistreatment they endured.

I contend that if young Black men knew what Black women of their past had to deal with, they would not want to disrespect them. They would not call their women bitches, whores, and sluts. If they only knew the names, their great-grandmothers had to endure. They would not beat their women if they knew how badly white men beat African American women. There is never a reason for a Black man to strike his mate; they have been beaten enough. Raise yourself above the ignorance that perpetuates abuse.

The plight of the Black man is that he is destined to relive his past because he refuses to acknowledge it, face it, and learn from it. I am grateful for every Black man who has taken the initiative to seek this knowledge. Knowledge is power. What will you do with the power you have been given?

It would not be hard for a young Black man to pull up his pants if he knew that the police harass more Black men because of their appearance than any other race of people. It would not be hard for him to pull up his pants if he knew it was a sign of his availability to other men. We must learn from the mistakes of our past. I think that the Black man should know where he comes from and what happened within the boundaries of his race four to five hundred years ago.

He should also know what happened to his family forty to fifty years ago. Because what happened then has set in motion the course of his life today.

You have to be willing to ask the hard questions. Questions like, why is my family living in the projects today? Is it because we had nowhere else to go, or was it because we allowed ourselves to become comfortable receiving rental assistance from the government? Why was my mother a single parent? Was it because my father was not ready or prepared to be a father? Or was it because my mother was never properly trained to be a wife or a mother? Why did my father leave my mother and me? Was it because he did not love us, or was it because he could do more for us by leaving the house than he could if he stayed? All of these are valid questions that deserve honest answers.

All these questions should plague our minds until we arrive at valid answers. In addition, the answers we seek can only be found in the knowledge of our past. Keep looking to know. Search your history, not just Black America's history but your bloodline's history. Your family history can unlock many of the closed doors in your life. Know who you are by knowing where you come from.

CHAPTER 8

UNITY

Unity is defined as the state of the condition of being one. This definition proposes that there is a place or a condition where more than one person, place, or thing can be brought together to formulate one person, place, or thing. So then, following the definition, one could believe that Black men and women can become one. However, there would need to be a place where this could become a reality; not a place that can be located on a map, such as a city or an arena, but a place in the minds of Black individuals. We must become united in our minds by pursuing one purpose and having the same agenda. The only way the minds can become united is by teaching individuals to pursue the same thought process. We must unite the minds.

"The reason why the world lacks unity, and lies broken and in heaps, is because man is disunited with himself."
- Ralph Waldo Emerson

In this quote, Mr. Emerson suggests that the world is not experiencing unity, because man himself is not united within. I concur with Mr. Emerson's evaluation because I hold to the Biblical perception of mankind. The Bible teaches that man is a threefold being. Man is a spirit that lives in a body and possesses a soul. Until a man is united with himself, he will never be able to unite with anyone else.

Until recently, we have dealt with ourselves in the flesh. I know this may sound a little out there, but follow me. For many of us, the only thing we know is the house we live in, but you exist in a completely different realm. Your spirit is the essence of who you are, and if you fail to connect to your spirit, which, by the way, is always in pursuit of spiritual things, you will miss your guidance. As a result, you become soulish and emotionally led individuals, being led by what or how your feelings lead or mislead you. Your feelings are motivated by many different things; surprisingly, food, chemistry, the moon, and so many different things dictate your feelings.

Many relationships have failed because they were entered into by individuals who felt something, and they allowed those feelings to give them a false sense of security. You must proceed past the feeling and find the logic behind a relationship, some type of commonality. However, you will advance through life much easier by being united within yourself.

So then, it becomes imperative that Black men begin uniting within themselves so that they can unite with their fellow men.

Unity itself has been a detached enigma, a mystery of sorts, especially within the African American populace. It's one of those things that is often talked about but never really attained. This is why it is imperative that we undo the web of separatism that has held on to us. When Black individuals efface the stigma of division that has clung to this race like a leech, they will be empowered to rise to the prominence afforded to all good Americans.

However, there still remains a problem. How do we erase the stigma? How do we change the statements that are made about Blacks when they move into a new community, "There goes the neighborhood"? What can be done to show our white neighbors that they don't have to move out because Blacks start moving in? Seemingly, it never fails: a Black family moves into a neighborhood, and all of a sudden, you begin to see "For Sale" signs throughout the neighborhood. How can we change the minds of individuals who refuse to sell or rent to the Black populace because their property value allegedly goes down when we move in? Can this possibly be true?

Black man, you have the ability to change it by becoming acquainted with yourself. You must look at yourself and like what you see. See yourself being full of potential to excel above every obstacle. Stop seeing the glass as half empty, but see it half full. Allow yourself to be empowered by who you see every day. Every morning, look in the mirror and see the only individual who can determine your destiny for that day. Empowering yourself by liking what you see is to instill in yourself pride. That will happen when you see yourself differently.

You can no longer see yourself living in the ghetto, even if you do live there. You must see yourself living in the complex of opportunity, so opportunity can knock. It is not where you live; it is what you do with where you live. Begin to nurture within yourself a sense of pride. Have pride in everything you have, and you will learn to respect it.

You can no longer see yourself walking through the corridors of darkness; in the darkness, a conflict exists. When you walk in the dark, you tend to mistrust everything around you. When you walk in the dark, an element of fear encompasses you. Do not allow yourself to remain in the darkness of conflict. Walk in the light. Jesus said in the Holy Scriptures of St. John chapter 8, verse 12, "Then spake Jesus again unto them, saying, I am the light of the world: he that followeth me shall not walk in darkness, but shall have the light of life."

You must see yourself in the light of life so that you might live in His peace. If you experience His light, you will have His peace. This will assist you in having unity within yourself. In doing so, you will believe that you can coexist and work with other Black men harmoniously, establishing the trust factor. Trust is needed for the development of unity. Unity can only be a reality when individuals have mutual trust in one another.

There are walls between you that are preventing the promulgation of unity. Tear this wall of ignorance down and see who is on the other side. This wall was not built by you. It was established during our enslavement. We were taught not to trust anyone but our slave masters, and this has existed for hundreds of years. This wall of ignorance has perpetuated and maintained distrust, hatred, and anger between members of the Black race. However, just as the Berlin Wall, a wall of hatred and division, was brought down and avenues of communication were opened, we must allow the walls of separation and ignorance to come down.

These seeds of discord that have been sown in your heart from centuries past are destroying any hope of peace and unity. Seeds that created animosity for your brother have created death for you.

During the years of slavery, our ancestors were taught to fear their brothers because of the color of their skin. Seeds of discord were sewn deep into their hearts, seeds that produced animosity for dark skin blacks and light-skinned blacks. The dark skin brother was taught to fear and distrust the light-skin brother, because he would inform the slave master of the plans of the other, and vice-versa. We see these things still existing today in our land. The seeds must be destroyed.

Tear up the fallow ground of your heart and reseed peace. It will not happen overnight, but if you reseed, it will happen. Remove any weeds of hurt and pain, things that might present themselves as being a hindrance to you trusting your fellow man. Give every Black man a chance to show you his character. Some will fail, but many will surprise you with their level of integrity. Establish lifetime relationships. And with these tools in place, we will stop fearing one another. Then trust can surface, and you can and will be able to release the fear of being destroyed, hurt, or mistreated by your brother.

America is a conquering nation, and it is full of conquering people. As a nation, we conquer our enemies, our financial woes, land, and anything else that presents itself as a nemesis. Unfortunately, this is not a status willingly offered to Black persons of America. For centuries, we have been forced to accept whatever has been given to us. We are beginning to see change but still have a long way to go. This certainly is not an attack on America. I love this country and am proud to be an American. Nevertheless, America must be proud to have me as an American.

The Black man desires to be a conqueror. Not in the sense that we look to take a nation, but we have a desire to conquer slavery that still exists. We no longer wish to be slaves of the system. The Black men that I have spoken to do not want to be herded into five of the southernmost 50 states of America. We want to conquer the barriers that prevent us from moving into any area we choose to live in. We want to be a part of America, with all the same chances, choices, and privileges offered to other Americans. The Black man must be allowed to play on the same field as our counterparts and receive the same rewards for winning or losing the game. We want to play the field that is not controlled by the influences of the powers that be. Therefore, we must become united as a people to conquer and possess.

Before any of the things I have mentioned can become a reality, Black men must cry. There is an urgency to this time of crying, because the road of destiny is bringing the Black man back to a time seen before in his history. I am beginning to see slavery resurface. Segregation is being discussed. Oh, it may have a different face, it may come with different clothes, but slavery is still slavery. If these issues are not dealt with, the Black man of today will respond differently than he has responded in the past. Unfortunately, the result will be much different. We were promised forty acres and a mule; all we got was a shack and a good swift kick from a mule. As a result, we find ourselves in a dilemma. There is an answer.

CHAPTER 9

QUEENS LIVING AMONGST US

A queen is the female ruler of a nation, usually by birth, or she is the wife or widow of a king. Often, a king doesn't come into his reign until he has taken a queen. The African American woman is one of the greatest assets the African American male can have in his corner. I would imagine that there are other women on the earth who are strong, powerful, and resourceful. However, I have knowledge about African American women. And as far as I am concerned, she is one of the greatest creations fashioned by the hand of God. She is strong in the sense that she does not give up when faced with life's adversities. She's powerful because she has a creative instinct, and I don't mind saying it. She is beautiful. She is a Queen when allowed to be.

The African American woman can make it appear as if the sun is shining even when the rain is falling. She has the power to birth a nation from her loins. From her wisdom and fortitude, she produces princes and princesses. She is rich in love and abundant in ability. There is nothing that she cannot do. She is like the eagle; she sores in her glory. She is like the elephant; she can carry the greatest burden. She is like the chameleon; she adapts to her environment.

When God created the Black Woman, He created her for perfection. Yet, there is a chink in her armor. A flaw as it were, she is one of the most misunderstood creatures on the planet. Most Black males fear her because of who she can be. The Black man can't understand her, and she can't understand him.

Understanding the Black female is actually simple. She is adaptable, and that is it, she knows how to adjust to whatever situation she finds herself in. As a race of people, we do well to learn from the African American woman. She is a force that is irreconcilable when pushed to her true place. My Black sister, hear me if you can. We need you.

Black man, cry until that Black woman standing beside you feels your true heart. You have hid it long enough. She has the ability to transform you. Within the character of the Black woman is a hidden trait. She can be who she needs to be. That is one of the reasons so many men are not being who they need to be. Let us consider, you can not be the king you desire to be until you recognize the need for your queen.

Let's go back briefly to Black Buck Syndrome. When the Black woman was enslaved, she transformed into a superwoman. She was forced to withstand an onslaught of abuse and survived. She withstood atrocities that was created to subjugate her and her offspring. Wherein the woman was created to stand beside her man and be his helpmeet, she was reconfigured due to her circumstances and often became his enemy. This created the woman that we see today, powerful yet reconfigured. She is now a woman who stands without a man.

I know many eyebrows are rising right now but wait. Let's really look at the woman of today. She is powerful, independent, and aggressive. There is nothing wrong with any of these character traits. However, all of these traits have been created due to her most dominant character trait, survival. Women today have a can-do attitude that says, 'If you can't do it, watch me. I'll show you how.' This has added to the present condition of the Black man. Because of the past, women are more independent now than ever before. I do not think that this is a bad thing. However, it is an issue that must be addressed.

The average Black female has, at one time or another, said I don't need a man. Whether it was about a job getting done or a child being raised, it has been said. She has adapted and learned how to survive without the man. She works and pays her way. She raises her children and has become the provider, protector, nurturer, disciplinarian, the total package. And for this, she is to be commended. However, this state of being has perpetuated the condition of the Black man.

The condition is this: Black men are not in the home. Therefore, the void experienced during slavery is the void we sense and experience today. It takes a Black man to raise a Black son. There are certain things that young Black men need deposited into their lives that only a Black father can teach them. Young Black girls need a strong Black father to love them. This will stop them from looking for love in all the wrong places.

A young Black girl needs a strong Black father because of her strong character. She needs the firm hand of a Black father to guide her through puberty and bring her into her womanhood. These statements do not negate the role of the mother. They only affirm the need for the father. He cannot be soft or weak. He must be allowed to be a man.

We often see men brought into families that are already existent. Woman, you must trust him enough to allow him to discipline your children, or you don't trust him enough to be in your home. Give him his authority, and by doing so, you give him his strength.

Black woman, the Black man is weak because you have not demanded of him responsibility. Now, by demand, I do not mean by yelling and screaming, but by your demonstration of your weakness. Let that man know that you need him to be a husband, supplying you with love and affection, offering you protection from the enemies of a successful life, and meeting all your needs. Help him see and understand the needs of the children. They need a father. He must feel the need.

For a man to be a man, he must be confronted with his woman's need to be provided for and protected. This is his character. He has been wired to protect and provide. He feels he serves no purpose in the relationship without that being presented to him. However, it must be done respectfully. You cannot challenge his manhood by telling him what he is not doing. You must show him how much you need him to do and continue doing.

Black woman, if your man doesn't have a man to teach him how to be a man, then you must help him, not by belittling him, but by reinforcing the right actions. Support his efforts, reassure him of your love and your confidence in his ability to love, provide, and protect. Remind him that you are what you are because he is who he is.

Further, let him cry. I am not suggesting that you turn your man into a baby. Neither am I suggesting that you allow him to remain immature. I mean allow him to pour out his heart to you and express his weaknesses without fear of it being used against him. By doing this, it will allow him to expose his insecurities and weaknesses to you. It will give you the opportunity to make him the king he should be. Beau-

tiful queen, accept my acknowledgment of who you are and
be just that.

CHAPTER 10

MARRIAGE

Marriage in America is under attack from a source unknown to the leaders of our times. The source's origin is unknown to many and, therefore, cannot be fought by the political machinery. The fear that has kept our politicians from speaking against the demise of holy matrimony stems from the same source. What is this source, you ask? It is the enemy of God.

The sanctity of marriage has been brought into question by radical groups, who, under the pretense of civil liberty, have allowed Satan, the god of this world, to lead them down a path of apostasy. How unfortunate for this nation because we have become much like Sodom and Gomorrah of the Bible. There appears to be no answer as to why 35% of Americans between 24 and 34 have never married, and the number is even greater among African Americans, and yet, we have movements fighting to legalize homosexual marriages. I am convinced that a Holy war has begun, and we are unaware. The enemy of God is fighting the Church, and the mirror of the Church, the family, is not on the front line. Satan is fighting the family.

Marital therapist and radio talk-show host Audrey Chapman worries about tomorrow; "African Americans are the most unpartnered group in America. Census figures show that 35% of Americans between 24 and 34 have never married. For African-Americans, that figure is 54%." Karen S. Peterson, a reporter for USA Today, stated, "Census Bureau statistics show that in 1998, 11.7% of Blacks aged 18 and over were divorced, compared with 9.8% for the general population."

This is alarming and very well should be. As long as we are not seeing Black men and women engaging in marriage, we will continue to see the moral decline of the Black family. Moral dilemmas exist because of the many children born outside the marriage bond. Children raised without the family structure are growing up to be individualists. So, then, even though it is out of ignorance, they are perpetuating the Black Buck Syndrome. Women who feel they don't need a man, men who flee the love of their women and children, and children who are raised in single-parent homes.

Chapman believes "the sexual revolution of the last two decades has wreaked havoc on black relationships." Young Black women now spend years getting an education and building a career. When they finally turn to the thought of settling down, they find a small pool of marriageable Black men. "Because available women so far outnumber them, many Black men often say they see no reason to make long-term commitments," Chapman says. "They feel it's safer to couple for the moment and move on."

The state of marital bliss is veritably nonexistent. Most young people who have reached the age of marriage are fearful of approaching because of the plethora of failed marriages in their view. Men and women have seen so much because of the threat of failure. It is hard to see a marriage of twenty or thirty years end up in divorce court, only to find that the only reason they stayed together so long was because of children born into the marriage.

There are many reasons why marriages fail. However, one of the main reasons for so many failed marriages is the lack of training and understanding between the man and woman. Until now, we have viewed marriage as a contractual agreement. However, it is slightly different than that. It is more of a covenant, a commitment, and so now we see the problem.

When a Black man thinks of a covenant, a commitment, or any type of situation that invokes a promise, he backs away or approaches it cautiously because of an inherent lack of trust. The Black man has been lied to, conned, and cheated so often that he cannot find the place of covenant in his heart. So then, when and if he enters the marriage, for the most part, he enters under false pretenses. What can be done to remedy this?

There is a remedy. However, it must be considered from a different aspect. A plateau of trust must be established. The woman he desires to marry must build within herself a place where the two of them can build trusting relationships. I say the woman because his woman will be the only one with the ability to convince him to trust again. The man, however, will have to be willing to trust again. This in no way concedes that the woman doesn't have the right to have trust issues. However, the woman has within her a nature that allows her to heal quicker than the man.

Even with high divorce rates, there is better news. Although many experts say the Black divorce rate outpaces that of whites, the General Social Survey (GSS) finds the two groups are quite close. About 36% of Blacks have divorced, compared with 34% of whites, says Tome White with the GSS, funded by the National Opinion Research Center at the University of Chicago. So, there is hope that Black families can turn the tide and begin rebuilding the institute of marriage.

CHAPTER 11

DEAL WITH "IT"

This statement, "Deal with it", is one that is heard mostly in sarcasm or rebuke, which in that context is simply saying there is nothing you can do about it. However, we need to look at "it". Before we bring this book to an end, there is one other thing to discuss. Many times in a relationship, it's difficult to determine who is at fault in any given situation. In their attempt to fix problems, men and women will create "it".

An "it" is the name of something you don't want to give a name. To give "it" a name means someone will have to accept responsibility for the present conjecture. So leave it unnamed, and no one will have the burden of saying I'm sorry first. However, until you address the "it" in your personal life, you will never be the man or woman, for that matter, you are supposed to be.

I know you've heard of "it". It is the first word in most excuses. "It's your fault", "It wasn't me." Even, "It's always me." And finally, "I don't want to deal with it."

The "it" in your life can prevent you from reaching the pinnacle of success designed for you. There is always an "it" in all of our lives. Whether you empower or destroy your "it" remains to be seen.

The "it" is whatever issue you have that prevents you from being honest with yourself, the issue that eventually becomes an emotional crutch upon which you depend. Your "it" is the internal touch point that causes conflict. What is that thing that lives in you that, whenever it is touched, causes you to react? If you can figure that out, you have won half of the battle.

Your internal touch point can be a past issue, abuse, or an area of inferiority. But, whatever "it" is, face it, confront it, and be healed of it. By facing it, you acknowledge you have it. By confronting it, you can address it, and then you can be healed of it. This area of life causes and even creates issues in many areas of life.

For example, if there has been abuse in your life, you will tend to abuse others. Therefore, if you are in a relationship that shows violent tendencies, you could possibly be dealing with someone who has experienced violence, or you could have experienced it as a sign of love and feel like you're not loved unless you see the violence. Depending on how you deal with it, the "it" will either cause you to act out or withdraw.

The Black man, as a whole, has an internal touch point. The abuses that were tolerated as a race have caused the race to act out. Some by implementing violence and abuse, some by withdrawing into a shell of excuses. It is my hope that by helping Black men to face the fact that these violations have taken place and are still going on, they will lunge forward and jump to the second level, the level where you confront "it."

The need for confrontation is desperate. In an earlier chapter, I stated that Black men don't like confrontation. However, I did not say that confrontation is impossible for Black men. Look at yourself and determine whether you are acting out or hiding. If you are one of the many Black men who are acting out, whether it is through outward displays of violence or ongoing abusive relationships, confront yourself. Perhaps you have hidden within yourself and refuse to have a voice in any situation. Determine which one and confront it so that you may be healed.

Black man, you do not have to be violent to prove your manhood. You must believe that one of the reasons you are where you are is the fact that abuse and violence only spawn greater abuse or violence. The fact that you can knock someone out simply suggests you can fight. It doesn't mean you're a man. You don't have to be violent towards your woman or your family. They will love you because you love them. And, if they can't, it is because they have experienced the same violence. Love them. Be strong and show stability. They will see that your love is strong enough to overcome the violence of all parties concerned. Deal with "it", whatever "it" is, and make the necessary adjustments. God is faithful and will help you make the changes.

DR. PAUL J. PORTERFIELD

As a Black man and leader in the Black community, my heart bleeds for all men, my race specifically. It is my hope that this book helps you become the man you are supposed to be, the king, and the leader in your family and community, regardless of race, color, or creed. It will require an effort on your part, a willingness to see yourself, your family, and your community and endure the pain of what you see. But don't stop there; avail yourself of the help being offered.

Watch for the next book, *The Absent Man*, visit the **The Absent Man** conference when it comes to a city near you, and become a part of **The Absent Man** chapter in your community. These aids will help you become "present and accounted for".

I look forward to seeing you at the top. I love you.

Be blessed!

ACKNOWLEDGMENT

I would like to acknowledge God, who opened my eyes, my wife, Angela, who stood with me during the process, my daughter, Chardane, who helped me to stay the course, and Dr. Nyisha D. Davis, my publisher, who wouldn't let go.

WHEN A BLACK MAN CRIES

References

Goodreads.com. (2024). Es'kia Mphahlele > Quotes > Quotable Quote. Retrieved from https://www.goodreads.com/quotes/8105681-black-man-cleans-the-streets-but-mustn-t-walk-freely-on

Kidspattern.com. (2024). Black. Retrieved from https://kidspattern.com/color-palette/color/black/#:~:text=Black%3A%20the%20very%20darkest%20color,light%3B%20the%20opposite%20of%20white.

Bibleportal.com. (2024). Qoute by C.H. Spurgeon Quotes. Retrieved from https://bibleportal.com/bible-quote/hope-itself-is-like-a-star-not-to-be-seen-in-the-sunshine-of-prosperity-and-only-to-be-discovered

Britannica.com. (2024). Slavery. Retrieved from https://www.britannica.com/topic/slavery-sociology

Collinsdictionary.com. (2024). Public Demand. Retrieved from https://www.collinsdictionary.com/us/dictionary/english/public-demand

Jones, Quincy, 1933-. (1977). Roots : [the saga of an American family]. [Place of publication not identified] :A & M,

Clliffnotes.com. (2024). Emerson's "Nature" Major Themes. Retrieved from https://www.cliffsnotes.com/literature/t/thoreau-emerson-and-transcendentalism/emersons-nature/major-themes#:~:text=Spiritualization%2C%20hastened%20by%20inspired%20insight,man%20is%20disunited%20with%20himself.

Vocabulary.com. (2024) Queen. Retrieved from https://www.vocabulary.com/dictionary/queen#:~:text=A%20queen%20inherits%20the%20title,to%20the%20guy%20in%20charge.

Stormfront.com. (2024). Radio Talk-Show Host Worries About a Black Tomorrow. Retrieved from https://www.stormfront.org/forum/t273649/. Audrey Chapman worries about tomorrow.

Peterson, K. S. (2024) Black Couples Stay The Course. Retrieved from http://216.218.174.47/mel/rdivorceblack.html

Gss.norc.org. (2011). Retrieved from https://gss.norc.org/

ZCP

ZCP